Journey

Finding God's Purpose For Your Life

Lisa Dodson

Fiction Cove Publishing, LLC
Raleigh, NC

This book is a work of nonfiction. These accounts are from the author's perspective and memories, and as such, are represented as accurately and faithfully as possible. To maintain the anonymity of the individuals involved, some of the names and details have been changed.

Journey: Finding God's Purpose For Your Life
Copyright © 2021 by Fiction Cove Publishing, LLC All rights reserved.
ISBN: 978-0-9998917-7-3 (Ebook)
ISBN: 978-0-9998917-8-0 (Trade Paperback)
Cover Designed by: J.L Woodson: www.woodsoncreativestudio.com
Interior Designed by: Lissa Woodson: www.naleighnakai.com
Editing by Joy Campbell: www.joylcampbell.com and Lissa Woodson: www.naleighnakai.com

Without limiting the rights under copyright reserved above, no part of this publication may be reproduced, stored in, or introduced into a retrieval system, or transmitted, in any form, or by any means (electronic, mechanical, photocopying, recording, or otherwise) without the express written permission of both the copyright owner and the publisher of this book, except in the case of brief quotations embodied in critical articles and reviews.

For permission, contact Lisa Dodson at writergrl007@gmail.com

The scanning, uploading, and distribution of this book via the Internet or via any other means without the permission of the owner is illegal and punishable by law. Please purchase only authorized electronic editions and do not participate in or encourage electronic piracy of copyrighted materials. Your support of the author's rights is appreciated.

If you purchase this book without a cover, you should be aware that this book is stolen property. It is reported as "unsold and destroyed" to the publisher, and neither the author nor the publisher has received any payment for this "stripped" book.

All Scripture quotations are taken from the New King James Version®. Copyright © 1982 by Thomas Nelson. Used by permission. All rights reserved.

Journey

Finding God's Purpose For Your Life

Lisa Dodson

♦ DEDICATION ♦

For anyone who has ever found themself journeying down the wrong path in life. The discovery may be scary, and finding the one you are destined to walk is perhaps challenging, but you will make it. God is right there beside you. Waiting and willing to guide you.

♦ ACKNOWLEDGEMENTS ♦

To the Lord, my God. Thank you for providing me with the Spiritual gifts that I need to do my part in advancing Your Kingdom. Thank You for loving me, and holding my hand as I walked through this season in my life. In Jesus' Holy name, Amen.

To my family. Thank you all for continuing to support me, no matter the nature of the endeavor. I'm blessed to have you.

To Pastors Lynton and Judy Turkington and my family of friends at Celebration Church. Thank you for embracing me with the unconditional love and light of God's mercy and grace. My cup runneth over.

To Lissa Woodson (Naleighna Kai), for your literary vision and for establishing such a fantastic Tribe of authors for this series who genuinely love and inspire each other. Thank you for being my editor for this book and for pouring into my life in beautiful ways.

To Joy Campbell, thank you for being my editor on this project and for providing your excellent eye, keen author's mind, and insight.

To my ride or die friends. Thank you all for being my sounding board over the years, for being my support, my cheerleader, my fiercest protectors. I Love, Ya'll!

To Shawn Williams - Thank you for relaying God's message for this Series to Lissa. Without you, this project would not have been written at this point in time. Your obedience to the Lord's Word is why we all are here.

To my Tribe Called Success, Namakir, and Namaste, and CBLR author friends. My prayer is that each of you literary titans continue using the gifts and tools that God gave you as you embrace your journeys.

Lisa Dodson

"Some roads are littered with hopes and dreams. Others are swathed in nightmares and tears. When the sun dies, and the night grows teeth the path fades. Detours become destinies where wisdom pummels the traveler and the ground like hard rain. The only way out was in. Adversity like water recedes and a bend in the road appeared. The choice was hers: follow the road to deliverance or keep company with shades and shards of memory."

Stephanie M. Freeman, *Necessary Evil* and *Unfinished Business*

Chapter One

A Light in the Darkness

Naomi glanced down at the three graves spaced equally apart. The shadows were falling, and the sun would set soon. The wind swirled around her and blew the dust over her feet and sandals. Her gray scarf whipped against her face, but Naomi was oblivious. Caught up in her grief, lost in her pain, she stood motionless. Unexpectedly, Naomi's anguish rocketed out of her like a geyser. A scream echoed off the rocks, and silence fell surrounding her long after her mouth closed.

"How?" She shouted. "How in the world am I supposed to carry on without my husband, Elimelech? He was the love of my life. It's hard enough breathing in and out every day, but now my beloved sons, Chilion and Mahlon, are gone, too?"

Naomi turned her face toward the sky and threw her hands in the air. "Why not just open up a hole in the ground and let me jump in, Lord, because I can't imagine life without them." She wrapped both arms around herself protectively. "The big question of the day is, *why* do I have to?"

Naomi paused for a moment as if an answer was supposed to materialize.

"Why take them and leave me stuck in a land packed to the brim with pagans? Moab is no Israel, but what were we to do? Our people were dying of famine back home."

Her family's graves were marked by many small stones as opposed to a large one, so Naomi knelt down and began replacing the stones that had shifted.

"Should we have stayed, Lord, and died with our family and friends? We came to Moab because it was close by and because food, land, and work were plentiful. Was that our big sin against you?" Naomi asked as she worked. "That we left and didn't stick it out? Elimelech, Chilion, and Mahlon loved you as much as I did. They were faithful and followed your commandments to the letter. But now I've lost not one man to break my heart over, but three."

More silence.

Grief caused Naomi to lash out. She grabbed one of the rocks that she was about to place and threw it.

"How is this fair?" She grabbed another and lobbed it. "I loved him. He was my all. I wanted to grow old with him and bounce our grandchildren on our laps. Now that dream is gone. Have you judged us, and my family came up short? What woman could endure this much and not lose her mind?" Rock after rock sailed through the air. They landed in the dirt, on boulders, or in the grass. The physical exertion caused Naomi's breath to come out in choppy gasps. Sweat dampened her temples, and her chest rose and fell as she struggled to regain control. It was a lost cause. She used the back of her shawl to wipe the moisture from her face before going to collect some of the stones she had thrown.

"I'm no saint. But I have always lived a God-fearing life. I study the scriptures, pray fervently, and live a life of servitude to honor you, Lord. I resist the urge to focus on material things and my fleshly desires. Yet here I am. Husbandless. Childless. With no possibility of being blessed with more."

Naomi used her scarf as a makeshift wheelbarrow to carry the stones back. Dropping to her knees, her hand instinctively seeking her husband's grave while she worked.

"This is not how I saw my life stretched out before me. You are Jehovah Jireh—my provider. Our family has served you faithfully, Lord. Even here in our adopted home of Moab, we worshipped and prayed to you, not the Moabite god, Chemosh. We were outsiders in this pagan land. Foreigners and they never let us forget it, but still, we honored our heritage and clung to your commandments."

Naomi worked between the three graves, placing each rock with infinite care.

"What is our sin? Why have I been allowed to live and my beloved family was taken from me? Please, Father, I beg of you to tell me."

When she finished, she sat back on her haunches. "Tell me how I can repent for this great sin? Please, tell me what to do."

The tears plopped from her face onto the arid rocks—wet spots left in their wake. Suddenly, a hand gripped her shoulder. The touch startled her, but she was too exhausted to be afraid. Instead, she raised her head slowly, as if the effort alone was too much to bear. Her eyes swollen and burning from the vast amount of shed tears.

"Mom, what's wrong?" her daughter-in-law and Mahlon's widow, Ruth, knelt beside Naomi. She wrapped her arms around her mother and held on tight. "Are you ill? Should I go and get help?"

"No," Naomi said as her shoulders drooped. "I'm not ill. I'm heartbroken."

"I know." Ruth dabbed at the corner of her eyes. "I was so worried about you. Normally, you're home before sunset. I didn't know what happened to you."

"Something *has* happened," Naomi whispered, "I'm dead inside. I have nothing left. No male relatives to provide for me—or you and Orpah. We're a stone's throw away from poverty, Ruth."

"Mother, please don't worry about us. Come on, let's go home. Orpah will have dinner ready by now. It would help if you kept up your strength. You don't want to get sick."

The wind whipped around them as they walked, causing the two to huddle closer.

"What do I care?" Naomi said after moments of silence.

"Well, I care," Ruth replied. "And don't think Orpah and I didn't notice that you barely touched breakfast this morning."

Naomi shrugged, and they hurried the rest of the way in silence. When they arrived, it was to find Orpah pacing the floor, her expression alternating between worry and fear.

Removing their sandals, Naomi and Ruth washed their feet before reaching for a cloth to dry off.

"We're sorry we're late, my daughter."

"Where have you been?" She ran to the door and retrieved a thick piece of wood. "I found this and was about to come looking for both of you."

Ruth's eyebrows shot upward. "And what had you planned to do with that rod?"

"Whatever I had to," Orpah countered. "Chilion taught me how to defend myself." She spun the rod in her hand several times at various speeds. Then, she pressed it forcefully in front of her before bringing it to her side with a loud thump.

"Impressive." Ruth smiled for the first time that day. "You're going to show me how to do that."

Orpah returned the rod to its place by the front door. She visibly relaxed. "Deal."

"What will people think if they see you?" Naomi murmured.

"If they're smart, they'll think to themselves, 'Hey, that woman can give me a smackdown if I mess with her or her family.'"

"They'll also think you are ill-mannered," Naomi warned, wagging a finger.

"Mom, there are no men in the house. I'd say my manners are the least of our worries."

Ruth shot her sister-in-law a glance. "Orpah."

Her sister-in-law was instantly contrite. She rushed to Naomi's side, placing her hands between her own. "I'm sorry," Orpah said as she hugged Naomi. "I didn't mean to make you sadder."

"It's okay, sweetheart. And you're right. It's just the three of us now. I shouldn't have stayed out so late and worried you both. I'm sorry."

"Well, you're home now, and that's all that matters. Look," Orpah waved a hand to the table. "I've fixed dinner."

She placed the *morsel*, a flat, dense, and rough bread made from inexpensive grains, on a plate and set it on the table with a small jar of olive oil. Next, she sat three clay bowls of a lentil pottage on the table. The modest stew was dense and helped stave off hunger. Dried fruits complemented their meal.

Naomi blessed the food, after which Ruth and Orpah attacked it with gusto while Naomi moved the soup around in the bowl with her spoon.

"You don't like it?" Orpah fretted, her lips drooped into a frown. "I know I'm not as great a cook as you and Ruth, but I try."

Naomi leaned over and squeezed Orpah's arm reassuringly.

"Oh no, honey, your cooking is wonderful. I'm just not hungry. Truthfully, it's been a long day, and I'm wiped out."

Orpah cast her eyes to the dining table. "Are you sure?"

"I promise you. Now, all I want to do is go wash up, throw on my nightgown, and get to bed. But thank you for the delicious meal, my beautiful daughter."

A smile lit up Orpah's face as bright as the North star. "I'm happy to help out wherever I can."

"I know. You are such a blessing to me, and you took such wonderful care of my Chilion. For that, I am eternally grateful."

Sadness flickered in Orpah's expression for just a second before being replaced with another overly bright smile.

After Naomi lumbered from the room, Ruth shook her head. "You love to cook about as much as I love to clean up donkey dung."

Orpah rolled her eyes before giggling. "I have improved."

"I will hardly argue the point," Ruth mused. She stood and began clearing the dishes away.

"So, what's with the overly sweet nature tonight? What are you up to?"

"What makes you think I'm up to anything?" Orpah questioned. "I care what happens to our mother just as much as you do."

"I don't doubt it," Ruth agreed. "But I know all this death hasn't been easy for you."

"It hasn't been easy for any of us," she replied, glancing over her shoulder. "In fact …"

When she stopped, Ruth looked up. "In fact, what?"

Orpah waved a hand dismissively. "It's not important."

Ruth was across the room in seconds. "Too late for that, little Miss Sunshine. What's going on?"

"I can't say. I don't want to upset our mother."

Touching her hand, Ruth said, "Then tell me instead."

After a few moments, Orpah relented. "There's been talk that we're cursed."

Ruth frowned. "What? By who?"

"People."

"Yes, I got that. *Which* people?"

Orpah shrugged. "I don't know exactly. I just overheard people at the marketplace a few days ago, and when I turned around, they were gone."

"And you're just now mentioning it?" Ruth paced about the sparsely furnished room that held their dining table, a few chairs, and mats on the floor, so there wasn't much to bump into when walking.

"Ruth, what if it's true?"

Turning a piercing gaze on Orpah, she said, "It's not."

"But, I heard that we could be cleansed. If we pray to—"

"Don't you dare," Ruth said in a harsh whisper. She stood to her full height. "You will not defile this house, our father, husbands, or mother's name by going against the Word of God. Do you understand, Orpah? We are not those people anymore. We married Israelites, and when we did, we promised to embrace their way of life—*their* God."

"But what if—"

"There are no ifs. We made a promise. Don't you remember?"

Orpah nodded slowly. "Yes, I do."

"Then we must keep it. Now let's get some rest. Tomorrow is a full day."

Ruth kissed her sister-in-law good night and left.

After she washed, Ruth strode to the side of the house where she had slept with Mahlon. Taking a pallet out of a trunk, she unrolled it onto the floor. Fluffing the covers as best she could, she kneeled as Naomi instructed.

Ruth prayed for her husband, father, and brother-in-law, then her mother and Orpah. When finished, she crawled onto the mat and pulled the blanket over her body. Her muscles were tired from the day's work in the fields, but they had to eat. With their men gone, it was a struggle to sustain themselves.

In that respect, Naomi was right. Their means of support dwindled each day with no end in sight. Their situation had to improve, and fast. Ruth had no idea what the future held for them, but now was the time for one of those miracles that Mahlon used to say only the God of Israel could provide.

"He that is slow to wrath is of great understanding: but he that is hasty of spirit exalteth folly."

Proverbs 14:29 (NKJV)

Chapter Two

A Path Forward

A visit to town was the highlight of the week. Vendors sold vegetables, honey, roasted nuts, clothing, livestock, and household goods in the marketplace.

Ruth bartered for some salted fish and cheese to go with dinner, while Naomi and Orpah took care of the other items on their list. With her task complete, she wandered over to the woman selling textiles. A blue and white striped tunic caught her eye. It was nicer than anything she owned. Unable to help herself, Ruth allowed her fingers to roam over the soft surface—a far cry from her everyday clothes.

"There you are," Naomi said, walking up with a basket full of supplies. "I wondered where you were." Her gaze followed Ruth's hand. "Oh my, that's lovely."

"Yes. Yes, it is," Ruth agreed.

Naomi raised her voice to be heard over the multitude of people rushing around. "Let's get it for you."

"Oh, no, we can't afford that. I'm content to stand here and touch it." Ruth spotted the seller's look of disapproval.

"Let's not make a habit out of it," the old woman grumbled.

"Forgive me," Ruth quickly apologized. "But, if you don't mind, can I stare at it for a few moments? It truly is an exceptional cloth."

The woman's expression instantly softened, and she beamed at the praise.

"Yes, of course. Take your time." She stepped back to give Ruth some space to ogle. Naomi moved away to speak to a friend as Orpah stopped at Ruth's side.

"Oh, Ruth, it's gorgeous. You should get it."

"Certainly not. It's too expensive." Ruth backed away from the bin. She took Orpah by the arm and walked down a different path. Feeling only a twitch of disappointment, Ruth acknowledged that was a far cry from the full-blown sadness that used to come over her when she thought about not being able to spend money. Fine linens, flawless jewels, and leather sandals were her old life. That was before she fell in love and married Mahlon. It felt like a lifetime ago.

There's no need to look back now. Ruth could imagine what Naomi would say if she were there. She chuckled to herself. *Ah, progress.*

Ruth caught up with her family. As they turned a corner, an impeccably dressed woman stood in the middle of the road. Her back was to them as she held court with two other ladies. With their path effectively blocked, Ruth opened her mouth to ask them to step aside, but the rich woman suddenly dissolved into laughter.

"I tell you, the family barely has a roof over their heads. It's such a shame that Naomi selfishly holds Ruth and Orpah back. They're still young enough to find new husbands. Of course, they've married foreigners and denounced our ways, so they aren't good enough for my darling boys, but I'm sure there are men of less noble birth who would be all too happy to take them to wife."

The woman motioned to her garment for effect. "Naturally, the first overhaul needed is a new wardrobe. Goodness, I've seen better clothes on beggars in the streets."

"You shouldn't say that," another friend cautioned. "It's not polite."

"That may be true, but heavens, have you seen them? They look like vagabonds." She laughed, with one hand pressed to her bosom. "But, in all fairness, with a complete makeover, they could be redeemable. You'd think that God of theirs would do a better job of providing for His people."

The woman laughed loudly at her wit. The fact that her friends were silent went completely unnoticed. When she finally caught their expressions and that their gaze traveled past her shoulder, she spun around to find Naomi, Ruth, and Orpah staring at her in shocked silence.

She registered a second of embarrassment and regret before pride kicked in. "Don't give me that look," she said in a haughty voice. "Was there one thing I said that wasn't true?"

Naomi placed herself in front of her daughters and stared the woman down. "I'm astonished how far your rudeness travels around this village. You smile in our faces yet gossip behind our backs with the ease of a striped hyena digging up tombs to dine on corpses. If this is the teaching from your stone idol, then I'm thankful to have no part in the blind worship of an idol that would approve your need to tear people down instead of using your energy to uplift."

"How dare you lecture me," the woman snapped. She sidestepped when her friend tried to grab her arm to keep her quiet. "Where is this God of *yours*, Naomi? Why do we never see him? There are no statues anywhere that depict him."

"Because He is invisible," Ruth replied, glancing up at the sky. "But He is always with us."

The woman snorted. "It's quite convenient that He is everywhere and yet nowhere."

"My God may be unseen, but He would never celebrate in His children's misery," Naomi gazed at the ridiculer with disdain. "Yet you seem to revel in it. If that is what your pagan idol teaches, then I'm glad we have no part in it. We may be poor, but we help anyone in need, love our neighbor as ourselves, and we don't harm anyone. That is our way. Can you say the same?"

Turning, Naomi grabbed hold of Orpah and Ruth and walked away as though she had all the time in the world.

"You sure told her," Orpah observed.

"I had no right to lose my temper," Naomi countered, trying to keep an even pace. "I should have let her catty behavior trickle away from me like water. The Word says, *"He that is slow to wrath is of great understanding: but he that is hasty of spirit exalteth folly."*[1]

"Come." She tugged her daughters along. "Let's get a special treat for dinner tonight. I saw some delicious fig cakes. We simply must get them."

Ruth wrung her hands and asked, "But mother, how can we afford it?"

"Let me worry about that," Naomi replied. "I have just heard the most wonderful news from a man in the market, and I can't wait to share it."

* * *

"I heard wonderful news from someone who's visiting from Bethlehem," Naomi said after dinner.

Orpah squealed in excitement and leaned forward. "Well, don't keep us in suspense, Mother. What happened?"

"The Lord has blessed his people in Judah. He has given them good crops again, daughters. The famine is over," Naomi cried as her eyes sparkled. "I've prayed so long for a miracle—and now it's here. There is light in the middle of my darkness. I can return to my homeland. I know that if I return there, all will be well."

"You mean *we*. We will come with you." Ruth glanced at her sister-in-law. "Right, Orpah?"

The silence was enough for them to hear the slight rustle of the wind. Several seconds went by before Orpah said, "I can't."

1　　　Proverbs 14:29 (NKJV)

Ruth leaned across the small table. "What do you mean you can't?"

"I'm going to stay here in Moab. My parents want me back. I can't say no."

"Yes, you can. It's simple," Ruth threw up her hands. "You say that you're going to Judah with the rest of your family."

"But, they are my family." Orpah sat back and mumbled, "My *real* family."

"It's okay, Orpah," Naomi interjected with a slight bow to her shoulders and disappointment coloring her tone.

"Oh, it most certainly is *not* okay." Anger flashed in Ruth's eyes. "What do you mean your *real* family? And just what are we? Skewered goat?"

Orpah's skin flushed in the candlelight. "No, I didn't mean it that—"

"Sure, you did. So, where was this real family all the times we went with no food, or we were barely able to pay our bills to keep the creditors off our backs, huh?" She spun Orpah around when she tried to look away. "I didn't see even one of your beloved family members come to help us in our time of need. Yet, they're the most important to you now?"

"Ruth, that's not what I meant. Don't try to put words in my mouth."

"Oh, don't blame me, widow of Chilion. Those words were already there—have been this entire time."

At the mention of her dead husband, Orpah stood. "You try and twist my words, and I don't appreciate it, Ruth. Like you never thought it was time to go?"

"I would never leave Mother," Ruth shot back. "We are all she has, and just like that, you'd throw away over a decade of love and family ties?"

"Enough," Naomi said in a low but firm voice. "There will be no voices raised in this house and no arguments. I know you both had families before marrying my sons. It's time you returned to them, my daughters. You should not anchor yourself to an old woman whose life is almost at an end—that would be a waste."

Ruth rushed to her side. "Why do you say that?"

"Because, it's true," Naomi's hands worried the sides of her tunic as she sat there.

"You aren't some nuisance that we plot to rid ourselves of the first chance we get. You're our most beloved mother. Orpah and I are Moabites, yet you have always loved us unconditionally and made us feel welcome—despite who I was and what I did in the past."

"That part was easy," Naomi replied lovingly. "Neither of you are those troubled and lost women you were before meeting my sons and learning about the God we serve."

She took both of their hands in hers and squeezed. "You and Orpah are the daughters I never had, so please allow me some liberties. I want you both to live—and prosper. You can't do that in a foreign country with people continuously pointing out that you're from a pagan land and are idolaters. They will scrutinize every wrong step you've ever taken. That's no way to live."

"But that's what you suffered," Ruth observed. "You came here with Elimelech and the boys. You didn't know a soul and worshipped the God of Israel, and yet you prospered."

"It's because we had the love of our God —and each other."

"And now you have us," Ruth insisted.

Naomi observed Orpah a moment before she nodded. "It's late. Let's not make any big decisions tonight. Let's turn in and discuss this tomorrow."

Naomi went to retrieve her bedding before blowing both women a kiss. She laid the covers by the fire. Once settled, she rolled onto her back and stared at the ceiling.

"Lord, please keep us safe from harm," she softly prayed. "This journey that we're about to embark on will be fraught with danger. There could be so much that goes wrong, but I have faith that you wouldn't send someone here to Moab to tell me that the famine ended in Jerusalem, if not to light a fire in me—to say to me that it's time to return to my homeland."

She closed her eyes and rolled over on her side.

"Protect us, Father. Keep us safe from harm. I repent of all the frustration, anger, and harsh words I said earlier about losing my family. I instead embrace your love and guidance in my life. Amen."

With a satisfied smile on her lips, Naomi fell into a deep sleep.

* * *

The next few weeks were a blur of activity for the women. Orpah had decided to journey to Judah with them. They sold all their livestock, except the donkeys, and what yield they could get from their crops. They had to travel light, so Naomi parted with everything in their house that could fetch a reasonable price. However, she kept a few personal items to remind her of Elimelech and their sons.

When it was time, they left Moab and journeyed along the road to take them back to Judah. By the time they reached the marker to leave Moab, Naomi had stopped. A strange look crossed her face. Suddenly, she lowered what she carried to the ground.

"Mother? What's wrong?" Ruth touched her arm. "Are you well?"

Naomi turned to face Orpah and Ruth. Her expression was unreadable.

"Go, return each to her mother's house. The Lord *deal kindly with you, as you have dealt with the dead and with me. The* Lord *grant that you may find rest, each in the house of her husband." So she kissed them, and they lifted up their voices and wept. And they said to her, "Surely we will return with you to your people."*

But Naomi said, "Turn back, my daughters; why will you go with me? Are there still sons in my womb, that they may be your husbands? Turn back, my daughters, go—for I am too old to have a husband. If I should say I have hope, if I should have a husband tonight and should also bear sons, would you wait for them till they were grown? Would you restrain yourselves from having husbands? No, my daughters; for it grieves me very much for your sakes that the hand of the Lord *has gone out against me!" Then they lifted up their voices and wept again; and Orpah kissed her mother-in-law, but Ruth clung to her. And she said, "Look, your sister-in-law has gone back to her people and to her gods; return after your sister-in-law."*

But Ruth said: "Entreat me not to leave you, Or to turn back from following after you;
For wherever you go, I will go; And wherever you lodge, I will lodge; Your people shall be my people, And your God, my God. Where you die, I will die,
And there will I be buried. The LORD do so to me, and more also, If anything but death parts you and me." When she saw that she was determined to go with her, she stopped speaking to her.[2]

Instead, she picked up her bags, and the two of them continued their journey. It was a long way, but they helped each other, rested when they could, and were always looking for any danger. Eventually, they came to Bethlehem. They were near exhaustion but rallied when they saw the entire town was excited by their arrival.

Naomi took in the scene for a moment. She breathed in the familiar scents that she had not smelled in decades.

Now the two of them went until they came to Bethlehem. And it happened, when they had come to Bethlehem, that all the city was excited because of them; and the women said, "Is this Naomi?"

But she said to them, "Do not call me Naomi; call me Mara, for the Almighty has dealt very bitterly with me. I went out full, and the LORD has brought me home again empty. Why do you call me Naomi, since the LORD has testified against me, and the Almighty has afflicted me?"

So Naomi returned, and Ruth the Moabitess her daughter-in-law with her, who returned from the country of Moab. Now they came to Bethlehem at the beginning of barley harvest.[3]

When they reached Naomi and Elimelech's old home, Naomi collapsed.

"Mother," Ruth cried. She rushed to her side and helped her up.

---

2   Ruth 1:8-18 (NKJV)
3   Ruth 1:19-22 (NKJV)

The house and grounds looked shabby from the outside, and the well was bone dry. Naomi imagined that the inside was ten times worse.

Ruth noticed her hesitation and said, "Why don't you sit for a moment. She handed Naomi the leather bladder that held the last of their water. Would you like a drink?"

Naomi shook her head and got to her feet. "No, bad news doesn't go down any better with water. Let's go in and see what we face."

They walked up to the front door and did their best to push the warped wood open. It took considerable effort. The door was damaged in a few places, and they could see through the wood.

Both stepped inside and then did a three hundred and sixty-degree turn around the room. Naomi spotted a rickety chair. She sat gingerly on its edge. When it didn't collapse, she relaxed on it with her total weight. Thanking God that they arrived without harm, Naomi prayed that they would be successful in their efforts to turn the dilapidated house back into a home. The place was ramshackle, dark, smelled horrible, and from the sounds of it, critters were in the house that she wasn't quite ready to meet. Still, it was all theirs, and they would have to find a way to make all the repairs on little to no money.

"I think I'll take that water now," she said.

"The LORD will guide you continually, And satisfy your soul in drought, And strengthen your bones; You shall be like a watered garden, And like a spring of water, whose waters do not fail."--Isaiah 58:11 (NKJV)

Chapter Three

An Unexpected Journey

"Mother, you and Mahlon always spoke of how loving and merciful your God was, but where is this mercy? Where are the abundant blessings your family spoke of so highly? We've been here several days, and this place doesn't look any better than when we started. We don't have any food left, and you are too weak to continue not eating properly. We need one of God's plans right now, or we'll starve to death."

Naomi hugged her daughter to her bosom. "Ruth, please don't despair. Remember when I was in the dirt by my family's grave? I was prostrate before the Lord, asking what more He could take from me and how I had nothing left. And you appeared before me. You helped me to my feet and provided help when I was feeling low and needed it most. Now I see that there *is* still reason to be grateful and have faith. It was in front of me the entire time."

"What was?"

"You, my daughter."

Ruth stared at her in confusion. "Me? I don't understand."

"You are one of my blessings. You and Orpah came to us and embraced my wonderful sons and our way of life, even though your own families and friends chastised you, and the god you worshipped was not our God. The two of you made Chilion and Mahlon so happy. Their father and I, too. Though neither of you had children, you provided much-welcomed peace to our family. I was wrong then to say that I didn't have anyone left. You and Orpah brought such love and joy into our lives. She hugged Ruth again before setting her away to look at her bewildered face. She touched Ruth's cheek.

"You are a wonderful, caring, loving, kind, and faithful daughter. Not once have you wavered or left my side. I know this has not been easy for you. We have so much work to do to make this place liveable, and we have no money or food to sustain ourselves, but my heart tells me that a path will be made clear. We didn't take this incredible journey back to Bethlehem just to suffer defeat at the hands of the enemy. The Torah says, *"The LORD will guide you continually, And satisfy your soul in drought, And strengthen your bones; You shall be like a watered garden, And like a spring of water, whose waters do not fail."*[4]

Naomi dropped to her knees. Ruth followed.

"Father in Heaven," Naomi cried, "please forgive my grieving tongue. I know that our circumstances, though dire, will turn around. You will never abandon Your children. I trust and believe that You will show me what we need to do and that You will provide for us because You do not fail."

A sense of peace flowed over Ruth as Naomi's words faded and the room grew quiet.

When Naomi glanced down to see Ruth looking with so much love and peace, she wept with gratitude because, at that moment, she had renewed faith that their situation would change.

---

4   Isaiah 58:11 (NKJV)

The following day, Naomi was in the house sweeping out the fireplace when Ruth rushed in.

"Mother, I went to get water and saw an older man walking down the road. He had a kind face and a staff he used to help him walk. He asked if you had returned from Moab. I told him that you had and that I was your daughter. That's when he smiled and said to wish you every happiness and that he was glad you have returned to your people."

"That was kind of him. But, what was his name?"

Ruth's mouth dropped open. "Oh no, I've forgotten. I was so excited to hear what he had to say that I completely forgot."

"Well, tell me, child. What did he say?"

"He told me that I could go out into the harvest fields and pick up what was left behind by those who are kind enough to let me do it. It is an ancient practice for widows, strangers, and orphans."

"Of course," Naomi replied, shaking her head. "It's called gleaning. I can't believe I had forgotten."

"I will do it."

"No, if anyone should go out to the fields, let it be me. These are my people. I don't want anyone giving you trouble."

"Mother, you have to take care not to overdo it. I am young, and it is my duty as your daughter to glean for our family. I don't care what people say to me for being from Moab."

"Very well, but you will need something to gather up the grain."

After Naomi provided a cloth sack that Ruth could tie around herself and capture the grain, she went off in search of a field. Watching her stride down the road with purpose, Naomi closed her eyes and said, "Thank you, merciful God."

Ruth left and went and gleaned in the field after the reapers. *"And she happened to come to the part of the field belonging to Boaz, who was of the family of Elimelech.*

Now behold, Boaz came from Bethlehem, and said to the reapers, "The LORD *be with you!"*

And they answered him, "The LORD *bless you!"*

Then Boaz said to his servant who was in charge of the reapers,

"Whose young woman is this?"

So the servant who was in charge of the reapers answered and said, "It is the young Moabite woman who came back with Naomi from the country of Moab. And she said, 'Please let me glean and gather after the reapers among the sheaves.' So she came and has continued from morning until now, though she rested a little in the house." [5]

Boaz went over and said to Ruth, "Hello, there. I see that you are new to my fields."

She glanced up and immediately shielded her eyes from the sun. "Why yes, I am."

"Welcome. You can glean here as long as you like. In fact, for safety, I caution you to stay here with us and do not go to any other fields. You should stick close to the other young ladies here gathering grain."

He pointed across the field. "You can harvest there with them. The women will treat you kindly, and the men have been warned not to trouble you. When everyone breaks for lunch, please come to the shelter. Oh, and there is water at the well, so make sure you stay hydrated."

Overcome with emotion, Ruth dropped to her knees. "Thank you," she exclaimed. "What could I have done to deserve such kindness from you? I am a foreigner."

Boaz smiled. "Yes, I know. But I have heard all that you have done for your mother-in-law since the death of your husband, Mahlon. I also know that you left your homeland, your father, mother, and all that you knew to journey with Naomi to live in a land of total strangers. I admire your courage."

Placing a hand on each arm, he helped Ruth to her feet. *"The LORD repay your work, and a full reward be given you by the LORD God of Israel, under whose wings you have come for refuge."* [6]

"Sir, I hope that I continue to please you and never do anything wrong or improper. Even though you don't know me, you have been very kind. I will make sure that I am always deserving of that kindness and that my actions never disappoint you."

---

5   Ruth 2:3-7 (NKJV)
6   Ruth 2:12 (NKJV)

Thanking him again, Ruth returned to her work, leaving Boaz staring at her with curiosity in his gaze.

An hour later, Ruth noticed that everyone lowered their gathering bags and headed toward the shelter. Reluctantly, she followed their lead.

Wiping the sweat from her face with the apron over her dress, Ruth went to the basins filled with water and washed her hands. She dried her hands with a cloth placed next to the container. Close by, a table was laden with food and pitchers of water. Unsure of herself, she padded by the groups sitting at the low tables on mats placed on the floor. She was about to go past Boaz when he called out to stop her.

"Please, come here and sit with us."

"I don't want to intrude," she hedged.

"You're not, trust me." Taking a plate off the table, Boaz handed it to Ruth.

"Help yourself to anything you see."

Ruth quickly surveyed the delectable-looking food before picking up a small piece of bread and placing it on her plate, along with some olive oil. Next, she added a bit of fruit. Boaz poured her a cup of water and set it down next to her place. He handed her the large bowl of roasted grain.

"This is delicious, thank you."

"My pleasure. There is always an afternoon meal available for my harvesters. I want you to promise me that you will help yourself whenever you are here gleaning."

She was about to protest, but Boaz leaned forward. "It is no inconvenience, truly," he said softly.

Ruth merely nodded and resumed eating. When she finished, she thanked Boaz again for the meal.

"Here," he said, gathering up some provisions. "Take some of these leftovers home to Naomi. I'm sure it's been difficult for the two of you since returning."

That's the understatement of the year. Ruth mused.

When she returned to work, Boaz summoned a few of his senior workers to his side. "And when she rose to glean, Boaz commanded his young men, saying, *Let her glean even among the sheaves, and do not reproach her. Also let grain from the bundles fall purposely for her; leave it that she may glean, and do not rebuke her."* [7]

Ruth was able to gather barley undisturbed for the rest of the day. She was elated that the satchel was filled to the brim when she beat out the grain that evening. As Ruth was leaving, Boaz stopped her again.

"How was your first day?"

"A lot nicer than it would have been at someone else's field."

Boaz smiled broadly. "I'm sure that's true. I'm happy that you had a successful day. Will you be here tomorrow?"

Ruth couldn't explain it, but her stomach fluttered under his frank gaze. "Yes, I will."

"I'm glad." He extended his hand toward her. "Forgive me. It dawned on me earlier that we have not been properly introduced. "My name is Boaz."

She shook it, marveling how well her hand fit inside his. "I am Ruth."

"It's a pleasure to meet you, Ruth."

"Likewise, Boaz. If there is anything that I can ever do to make up for your hospitality, please tell me."

"Just seeing that worried look on your face fade into a smile is enough."

Stunned, she watched Boaz vault onto his horse and gallop away at breakneck speed. It was moments before Ruth noticed that she was still staring. For the first in a long while, she felt relief. Their circumstances had changed so drastically in such a short amount of time. Thanks to Boaz.

After saying a prayer of thanks to God, Ruth allowed herself the indulgence of plastering a colossal grin across her face.

---

7   Ruth 2:15-16 (NKJV)

Chapter Four

Naomi Restored

"Mother, you will never believe what happened." Ruth sped toward Naomi, who was outside pulling weeds from old planting beds. Breathless, she handed over the food that Boaz had provided.

Frowning, Naomi asked, "What is this?"

"A gift from the man whose field I gleaned in today. And can you believe this?" She held out a bag brimming with grain. "I had to be careful running home. I didn't want to drop one piece."

"Where did you gather all this?" Naomi exclaimed. "May our Heavenly Father bless all those who helped you."

Raising both hands, Ruth declared, "He knows you—and everything about us."

"I'm not surprised. You'll see soon enough that nothing occurs here that the entire village doesn't know by nightfall." She smiled, then added, "Tell me his name, daughter. I will seek him out and thank him for showing us kindness."

"His name is Boaz."

"Boaz?" Naomi almost toppled over while getting to her feet. "Why Ruth, he's one of Elimelech's kinsmen. What a blessed turn of events."

"How so, Mom?"

"Boaz was doing well for himself when we left, but to own fields, he must be quite wealthy and influential in Bethlehem."

Smiling, Ruth said, "He had dozens of people working for him, and yet he was the nicest man I've met since we've been here."

"This is God's doing, Ruth. Here we are on the brink of disaster, and the Lord steps in and intervenes. This is wonderful, daughter." Naomi exclaimed with glee. "As a male relative, Boaz is obliged by law to do whatever he can to help us."

As if to prove her point, a man driving a large wagon came into view, followed by more men on horseback. When they reached the house, he hopped down and approached them.

"Greetings. My master, Boaz, instructed us to bring you these supplies and to fix everything that needs repairing on the house and outbuildings."

Naomi's eyes grew wide, and her hand flew to her chest. She watched in awe as one of the visitors led a goat past them, followed by baskets of food, cistern jars filled with water, and bales of hay.

"I can't believe what I see," Ruth said in awe. "Relative or not, why should he be so generous to us?"

A man stopped and handed her a basket overflowing with food. "It's just our way here."

Shaking her head in wonder, Ruth said, "I never saw such generosity in Moab."

Naomi hugged Ruth tightly. "Come, let's go inside and start finding places to put all of these things."

While Boaz's men worked on repairs, They spent the next few hours organizing the gifts they had received and thanked God for the timely arrival of the supplies, which coincided with Ruth's good fortune in the fields. The next day, Boaz came to the farm to visit.

Smiling, Naomi rushed over and clasped Boaz in a warm embrace.

"I was planning on paying you a visit. There are no words to thank you for all that you've done."

"Don't you dare try. It was my pleasure, I assure you." Boaz scanned the room from top to bottom. "The house is looking much better. My men did a good job."

"They did an excellent job," Naomi corrected. "You've saved us."

"You would have done the same if our situations were reversed. Besides, what good is having wealth if you can't spend it to help those you care about?"

He glanced at Ruth when he spoke. Naomi noticed the current that passed between the two of them.

"Interesting," she said under her breath.

Boaz tipped his head toward Naomi. "What did you say?"

"Oh, nothing of any importance. Won't you stay for dinner?"

"I would love to, but I have an important meeting in town." His gaze lingered on Ruth longer than necessary before he cleared his throat. "Goodbye, ladies."

Waving happily, Naomi turned and strode into the house. She was not surprised when Ruth entered right after.

Naomi went to the chest, where she kept her clothes and opened it. "We don't have much time. We have to act quickly, daughter."

"For what?"

"Boaz will be winnowing barley this evening on the threshing floor. We must make the most of the opportunity we have. First, you must bathe and then put on perfume. And here, wear this." She handed Ruth the blue and white dress she had purchased. Naomi's excitement was barely in check.

"Mother, this is the one from the market." She caressed the fabric between her fingers. "But how? Why?"

"I knew it would be useful one day, and I was right. You loved it, and I know it will look spectacular on you. I had to buy it for you, Ruth. And if I can read the signs correctly, my sacrifice will not be in vain. This dress will change your life forever."

Smoothing her hand over the front, she looked at Naomi. "I don't understand."

"Listen carefully. Go to the threshing floor, but don't let Boaz see you until he has finished eating and drinking. He will be in a joyous mood. Next, be sure to notice where he lies down and then go to him. Lie down at his feet and uncover them. Trust me, daughter, Boaz will tell you what to do."

"Are you serious?" Ruth replied in shock. She wasn't familiar with the custom but was confident Naomi would explain when the time was right. As she dressed, Naomi did her hair and relayed what the gestures she had suggested meant under their law.

Ruth's face was flushed pink, but from the confident look Naomi sported, she was positive things would work out according to plan.

* * *

Ruth did as Naomi instructed. She kept herself hidden while Boaz and his men winnowed the barley. They laughed and talked as they worked. Seeing him so carefree made Ruth smile. After they finished, everyone went to eat and drink. Squeezing her hands together nervously, Ruth continued waiting. Later that evening, Boaz was in an even better mood. When he got up, he carefully made his way to the far end of the grain pile in a quiet, secluded spot. It wasn't long before he fell asleep. Ruth remained where she was just beyond the threshing floor, hidden from view behind the treeline. She stayed rooted to her spot until some men left to go home and others found places of their own to lie down.

"Now's the time," she whispered.

Ruth crept toward Boaz and gave the sleeping men a wide berth as she moved closer to her destination. Her heart beat a steady staccato as she was afraid of being discovered, which made her slower and more cautious. Her stomach rolled around from her nervousness, but Ruth reached Boaz without incident. Lowering herself to the ground, she pushed his large cloak away from his feet before she laid down.

She closed her eyes and tried to get comfortable. A sigh of relief left her lips as Boaz remained immobile. *I don't know what will happen, God, but I will trust that all will be as Naomi said.*

After midnight Boaz stirred. When his feet bumped against Ruth's body, he turned over and sat up quickly. He peered at her in the darkness, clearly startled to find a woman lying at his feet.

"Who are you? What are you doing here?" he demanded.

"Please don't be angry. It is me, Ruth," she said quietly. "I have come to see you."

"What's wrong? Has something happened to Naomi?" Boaz shifted as if to rise, but Ruth's hand on his chest stilled his movements.

"Please, don't. Naomi is fine. I—I'm here because of you."

Boaz ran a hand over his stubbled jaw. "Ruth, let's talk. I need you to explain precisely what you're doing here at my feet."

Ruth turned her head to glance around. "Boaz, I thought my intention was clear."

"Not to me, it isn't."

She paused with uncertainty. "Mother told me that I was to spread the corner of your covering over me, and that it was a Jewish custom."

"It is," he said softly.

"She said that you would know what it meant."

"I do," he agreed. "I just want to be certain that *you* know what it means."

Ruth lowered her gaze. "It means that I am open to you being my kinsman-redeemer."

There were many emotions crossing Boaz's face, but Ruth missed them all. Finally, he tilted her chin up and peered into her eyes not once breaking eye contact.

Boaz squeezed Ruth's hand reassuringly. "If I am your redeemer it means that you are receptive to my offer of matrimony—are you?"

She nodded.

"I have to hear the words, Ruth."

"But, you haven't asked me."

He chuckled and shook his head, but didn't release her hand.

"Ruth, daughter of the late Elimelech and Naomi, will you accept my hand in marriage—will you be my wife?"

"Yes, Boaz. I will be your wife."

He searched her face a moment for something, but he didn't say what. Finally, he must have found it because he grinned and said, "Ruth, may the LORD bless you. "You are very loyal to your family. I thank you for not going to a younger man, whether rich or poor."

She hesitantly touched his shoulder. "You are kind, Boaz. You have a good heart, and I feel at ease when I'm with you. Peace is something that I have not had a lot of since Mahlon died."

Boaz stared at her a few moments. "Ruth, do you trust me?"

"Of course, I do.

"Then be at peace and don't worry. I will take care of everything. By now, everyone in town should know how virtuous you are. The only issue is that another relative is closer to Naomi than I am. Because we must follow the law, he will have the first right to redeem you."

Ruth started to protest, but Boaz touched the side of her cheek. "Have faith. Stay here with me tonight. I promise you will come to no harm."

"Of course."

"I'll talk to him in the morning. If he is willing to care for you, he will have the right to do so, and I must abide by his decision. But if he refuses, then as surely as the Lord is sovereign, I will marry you myself."

She bowed and hid the smile that wanted to break free. "I will do as you suggest."

"Good," he said, then grinned and took her hand and assisted her to stretch out by his side. A second later, he pulled his large cloak up to cover them both. "Rest easy, Ruth. The Lord has brought us together for a reason and our God does not make mistakes. We will place our trust in Him."

* * *

In the early morning, Ruth and Boaz awoke before anyone else. Boaz asked her to hold her garment out, and when she did, he lay six measures of barley on it.

"What is this for?" she asked, her eyes wide. "It weighs a ton."

"To take to Naomi. You must not go back to your mother-in-law empty-handed."

Seeing that Ruth was struggling, Boaz carried it most of the way for her.

Naomi was filling a water bucket from the recently fixed well when she spotted her daughter coming into the courtyard. She rushed to meet her.

"My goodness, what's all this?" she exclaimed, taking some of the grain from Ruth. "You walked from the threshing floor with this big load?"

"No. Boaz helped me. He wanted you to have this."

Delighted, Naomi motioned for them to go inside. Setting the grain down, she led Ruth to the table. "Tell me everything that happened. Don't leave anything out."

Recounting her night with Boaz, Ruth couldn't contain her concern. "Mother, what if your closest relative decides to adhere to Levirate law and marry me? He would have every right because I am the widow of Mahlon, and you have no other sons for me to marry and pass on Elimelech's inheritance, so as my kinsman-redeemer, he would be obligated to provide for you and me."

"It is true, Naomi confessed, wringing her hands together anxiously. "And Boaz would be powerless to stop it."

"But what then? I'll be stuck with a man I don't love."

"Then it's true?" Naomi beamed, and the corners of her eyes crinkled. "I haven't misread things. You love Boaz?"

"So much that I want to scream," Ruth gushed. "But what if I lose him because of this law?"

Naomi hugged her tight. "I know Boaz. He will not rest until he has sorted out this matter today. Oh, Ruth, you must have faith, child." Nodding sagely, she added, "I guarantee that at this very moment, he is making things happen."

"For I know the thoughts that I think toward you, says the Lord, thoughts of peace and not of evil, to give you a future and a hope." --Jeremiah 29:11 (NKJV)

Chapter Five

Only God Knows the Entire Plan

Now Boaz went up to the gate and sat down there; and behold, the close relative of whom Boaz had spoken came by. So Boaz said, "Come aside, [a]friend, sit down here." So he came aside and sat down. And he took ten men of the elders of the city, and said, "Sit down here." So they sat down. Then he said to the close relative, "Naomi, who has come back from the country of Moab, sold the piece of land which belonged to our brother Elimelech. And I thought to [b]inform you, saying, 'Buy it back in the presence of the inhabitants and the elders of my people. If you will redeem it, redeem it; but if [c]you will not redeem it, then tell me, that I may know; for there is no one but you to redeem it, and I am next after you.'"

And he said, "I will redeem it."

Then Boaz said, "On the day you buy the field from the hand of Naomi, you must also buy it from Ruth the Moabitess, the wife of the dead, to perpetuate the name of the dead through his inheritance."

And the close relative said, "I cannot redeem it for myself, lest I ruin my own inheritance. You redeem my right of redemption for yourself, for I cannot redeem it."[8]

It was customary in Israel to remove one sandal and hand it to the other party when deferring to someone else for a purchase. So when the other family redeemer drew off his sandal and handed it to Boaz in front of witnesses and said, *"You are witnesses this day that I have bought all that was Elimelech's, and all that was Chilion's and Mahlon's, from the hand of Naomi. Moreover, Ruth the Moabitess, the widow of Mahlon, I have acquired as my wife, to perpetuate the name of the dead through his inheritance, that the name of the dead may not be cut off from among his brethren and from his position at the gate. You are witnesses this day."*

And all the people who were at the gate, and the elders, said, "We are witnesses. The LORD make the woman who is coming to your house like Rachel and Leah, the two who built the house of Israel; and may you prosper in Ephrathah and be famous in Bethlehem. May your house be like the house of Perez, whom Tamar bore to Judah, because of the offspring which the LORD will give you from this young woman."[9]

* * *

Ruth paced the living area in Naomi's house, desperately trying not to crawl out of her skin. Hours had passed since she had parted with Boaz, and she had not received an update on how things were going.

I'm going to lose my mind, she told herself. What if Boaz failed, and I'm forced to marry someone else? That thought dropped Ruth to her knees in the middle of the room. With her hands clasped tightly, she prayed.

"Hi, Lord, it's me, Ruth. I know I shouldn't worry and that worrying

---

8   Ruth 4:1-6 (NKJV)
9   Ruth 4:9-12 (NKJV)

is a sin, so how about I say that I'm a little concerned about what might be going on right now. I've had such a journey to get to You, God. Which, of course, You know because You know all. I'm kneeling before You now, Lord, because I love Boaz. I want to become his wife more than I want anything in my life. Oh, except to rejoice in Your love and praise Your holy name, of course. Whatever Your will is, Father, it will be done, but could You please make it Boaz and not the other guy?" She closed her eyes extra tight. "Thank you, Father. Amen."

"Amen."

Ruth's eyes flew open, and she whirled around.

Boaz leaned against the wall near the front door, watching her.

She held her breath.

When his smile went supernova, Ruth shrieked with joy and rushed across the room to stand close to him.

"You did it," she stated. Tears stung her eyes and rolled down her face. "He agreed."

"Yes. We should thank God for His graciousness, for He has been very merciful this day."

"He certainly has. Oh, Boaz, I'm so happy."

Sweeping her into his arms, he spun her around. "As am I, my beautiful bride-to-be. That is if you will still have me?"

"There is nothing on Earth that can separate us now," she vowed. "What the Lord will join, let no man put asunder."

"Amen to that," Naomi said, coming into the room from outside. The bucket of water she had gotten promptly forgotten. "I am no longer Mara, but truly Naomi, for the Lord has made me pleasant once more." The three of them embraced each other and praised God for bringing them together and blessing their family.

* * *

Boaz and Ruth were married and soon had a son.

Then the women of the town said to Naomi, "Praise the LORD, who has now provided a redeemer for your family! May this child be famous in Israel. May he restore your youth and care for you in your old age.

For he is the son of your daughter-in-law who loves you and has been better to you than seven sons!"

Naomi took the baby and cuddled him to her breast. And she cared for him as if he were her own.

Then the women said to Naomi, "Blessed be the LORD, who has not left you this day without a close relative; and may his name be famous in Israel!" [10]

"Show me Your ways, O LORD; Teach me Your paths. Lead me in Your truth and teach me, For You are the God of my salvation; On You I wait all the day." [11]

* * *

There is so much we can learn from the book of Ruth. It's a short book, but it's packed with lots of spiritual nuggets: The importance of faith, family, humility, unwavering love, and recognizing that sometimes the path you're on may not be the one you're destined to walk.

Ruth embarked on a journey that would change her life forever. From the moment she met Mahlon, married him, and became a family member, she began living a different life. As a Moabitess, the Lord placed her on a path that Ruth would never have chosen for herself. Her trust in Naomi was unwavering, as was her desire to come to know and love the God of Israel as her Lord and Savior. And let's not forget Naomi. She was also about to have her predictable world turned upside down.

When the story began, Naomi was bitter, she was devastated over her losses, and she felt empty inside—broken. She didn't focus on what she had, two daughters that loved her unconditionally. Instead, Naomi told people to call her Mara, for she was bitter, and she felt that God had dealt with her bitterly. Her life path was as foreign to her as the land in which her family lived. Her journey to Moab was for safety, but the return to Bethlehem was for peace and redemption.

____

10   Ruth 4:14 (NKJV)
11   Psalm 25:4-5 (NKJV)

Chapter Six

A New Destination

"Do not remember the former things, Nor consider the things of old. Behold, I will do a new thing, Now it shall spring forth; Shall you not know it? I will even make a road in the wilderness And rivers in the desert."[12]

When I think of taking a journey, it's a lot more than going from one place to another. I think of the excitement involved in trying something new. The nervousness I feel when I'm stepping out of my comfort zone and stirring things up. I've always associated the word with a feeling of happiness and positivity. Still, there are journeys in life you find yourself on that you never expected to take or paths that you never expected to find yourself walking. The ones that you don't see coming, and therefore couldn't have planned.

When I recalled my wedding day on a chilly March afternoon twenty-five years ago, not once did I envision my journey leading to divorce after twenty-three years of marriage—and yet, here I am.

Ah, divorce. The dissolution of a promise that I made before God, family, and friends. Now, I'm two years into a path that I never dreamt I'd be walking. To me, divorce was more complex than death. At least with death, you grieve, you say goodbye, and there is closure. But with the end of a marriage, two people joined—mind, body, and soul—have been ripped apart. The two who became one are now legally back to being two. So yes, it felt like a part of me had gone missing. And if you still talk, see, or interact with the person you've divorced, that's a never-ending feeling of reliving a death each time you have to see that person again.

What made it harder was that we had attempted reconciliation—a second chance at salvaging a fractured relationship. However, I noticed that old patterns and habits resurfaced, which weren't healthy for either of us. Who wants to admit defeat? I certainly didn't. The ending of my marriage wasn't because the love wasn't there. It was. But, it wasn't enough to counterbalance the weight caused by the slow and steady drifting apart of personalities, values, ideals, and lifestyles. To put it plainly, my husband and I had become unevenly yoked.

"Do not be unequally yoked together with unbelievers.
For what fellowship has righteousness with lawlessness? And
what communion has light with darkness?"[13]

Even though by my husband's actions, I was given a get-out-of-the-marriage card, it was still hard to let the dream go. I found myself swimming in the treacherous waters of unanswered questions. *Why didn't we try harder? Why didn't I take a closer look at our differences before marriage? Were there warning signs I chose to ignore? What would my life look like from this moment on? How do I rebuild my life at fifty-one?* But, unlike Naomi, I was not bitter. I didn't question my

---

13   2 Corinthians 6:14 (NKJV)

circumstances, but there was one question that I wanted answered but was coming up with nothing but blanks.

I asked myself, *what was the point in getting back together to have things not work out?* It haunted me and made sleeping difficult. One night, my heart felt heavy. In desperation, I asked the Lord to please help me to relax so that sleep would come. After several nights of restlessness and bad dreams, all I craved was oblivion. What I received was a revelation.

It started as a dream that I was watching yet another front-row seat to my failed marriage. Then the whole picture shook in front of me and went pitch black. Next, an image of a man appeared before my eyes, and I knew two things. First, without a doubt, I was looking at Jesus. Second, I was wide awake.

The Lord will meet you where you are. He will come to find you in your time of need. And at that moment, Jesus stepped in the middle of my nightmare and disrupted it. I heard His voice clearly in my head. He told me that I couldn't carry other people's pain. They had to bear it themselves. Next, the Lord held out His hand. Though all I saw was a blinding light, I instinctively knew Jesus was offering me His heart. I just had to take it. A wave of calm that was tangible washed over me. My rolling stomach stilled, and the pain in my heart ebbed. That's when I opened my eyes to verify that I was still awake, and no, this wasn't a dream.

That experience was my wake-up call to let me know that I'm not just hanging out on earth under the radar of the Divine. I'm not drifting through life unnoticed. The Lord *knows* me. He knows where I am and how to reach me. My Heavenly Father knows what is going on in my life—at all times. And He cares.

That was a freeing thought, and with this newfound peace came the understanding that it was time to stop kicking the can down the road and let my marriage go. Though I'd moved out before and built a life that didn't include my husband, things didn't feel final. A connection remained. But this time, when I left, I knew in my heart that link was gone. The ties that bound us were irrevocably severed, and despite the pain, heartache, and loss, I *knew* I would be okay. I no longer needed my question answered because the "why" it hadn't worked out was now irrelevant. Why? Because the Lord lessened my pain and set me on a different path. He didn't allow me to dwell on the past and what was lost. Instead, the focus was on what lay in front of me.

"The Lord often leads us according to the needs of our heart, not always according to its desires." ~ Wayne Stiles

Do you sometimes wonder why the Lord allows us to go on such a long journey when we could've gone on a shorter one and arrived at our destination quicker? I do. But what I've found lately is that the Lord isn't working on the timetable that we are. Usually, if it's a long trip that we're on, God is using that time to change our hearts so that we will be ready for the destination when we arrive.

You may feel the trial you're going through is a wilderness, but the Lord doesn't leave us wandering out there alone. He didn't do that when Moses led his beloved Israelites out of Egypt toward the Promised Land, even when they complained and grumbled to Moses about wanting to return to their lives as slaves. God still provided a cloud by day to lead the way, fire at night, and manna from Heaven to eat. He provided for his people thousands of years ago, and he will provide for you today.

We have to trust that God's plans for us are better than our own. And that it's our hurt, pain, and doubt that hinder our ability to see past our current 'desert,' but the Lord is omniscient (all-knowing). So while I couldn't see past my failed marriage or trust that I would recover from my life tilting on its axis, He already knew the flip side of the coin.

New challenges and joys on the horizon awaited me.

However, I needed to be strong enough to embrace 'new' and what that meant. And those changes in my life began with a declaration that went something like this, "Lord, I've lived the last fifty-one years without You being at the helm, and we see how that turned out. I think it's time that I allow You to lead and put You first."

The thought of being alone and not part of a couple didn't bother me. I'm an introvert, so I never tire of my own company. One thing that surprised me about my newfound freedom was how fast friends and loved ones tried to get me back on the dating hamster wheel. Seriously? I'd just dove headfirst off the marital treadmill and wanted to breathe and enjoy my new life and figure out what to do next.

Despite people's advice to get back out there and begin dating again, I was in no rush. I wanted more than having a "plus one." Now was the time to reconnect with myself—do a complete overhaul from the inside out. I called it the 'Year of Lisa.' I gave myself time to learn what I liked, didn't like, and what my goals for my life would be. I made my health and personal walk with Jesus my priorities. My circle of life looked much different than it had for the past twenty-plus years.

Now, Jesus was at the center of my universe, and everything and everyone else would have to orbit around His presence in my life. Was it scary? Yes, change usually is. But I thought about Moses. He is one of the most well-known people in the Bible. He was a leader chosen by God to bring His people out of Egypt and into the Promised Land. The Lord used Moses to deliver miracles, signs, and wonders to Pharaoh to release God's chosen people, the Israelites. To deliver His people from the bondage of slavery. Was Moses ready to take on that role? Absolutely not. Did he willingly accept the mantle the Lord gave him? Nope.

Moses came up with multiple excuses to explain why he *wasn't* the man for the job.

He worried that he didn't have the ability, he wasn't a good speaker, he didn't have the authority for such an influential position, and finally, he flat out asked the Lord to send someone else. He thought these reasons were going to get him off the hook, and God would assign someone else the task He gave Moses.

Sowing fear and doubt that your abilities aren't good enough for God is Satan's tactic for keeping us from growing closer to the Lord. But you *are* enough. The enemy wants you to procrastinate and make excuses, but you can overcome those harmful black holes.

You *do* have power. It is bestowed from God himself to everyone that becomes a born-again believer and accepts Jesus Christ as their Lord and Savior. Christians receive the gift of the Holy Spirit. He dwells within all believers. But most importantly, God would never call you to an assignment and not provide you with all the tools you need to get the job done. That is not the type of God that we serve. He is a provider to His children—in all things.

For me, I had to stop worrying about what I couldn't do and put my trust in Him to have my back as he did Moses and everyone else He had called to action.

God walks every path before us. Sometimes, the road is rocky, the pieces broken, or the way unseen. But He is there. Focus on having the courage to walk a new path when presented to you because you are never walking it alone.

The promise of what would be superseded fear of the unknown, past failures, doubt, and pain in my life. Like my Biblical sisters and Moses, I had been gently and lovingly placed on a different path. The profound question at that moment was—what was I going to do about it? Embrace it? Or Fear it?

Moses Moment – *The last two years have been an uphill climb for me, but I know Jesus has been beside me, keeping me company, clearing a path ahead of me while simultaneously protecting my back. Have you ever tackled a challenge you didn't think you could manage, but the Lord brought you through? Say a quick prayer of thanks for Him never leaving your side on that journey.*

Chapter Seven

We Can't Fill God's Shoes,
But We Can Walk in His Footsteps

"For I know the thoughts that I think toward you, says the LORD, *thoughts of peace and not of evil, to give you a future and a hope."*[14]

So while it was true, one path I was on had ended, new ones were opening up. This reminded me of Ruth because the life she'd known had changed drastically, too. And similarly, her long journey to a new life in Bethlehem started with trusting God to have her back regardless of how many rocks littered her path along the way.

I also admired Naomi for her perseverance. Though she was heartbroken and suffered a significant loss, the Lord was still the center of her life. She wanted to walk in step with His word though she didn't always understand His plan. How could she? It was God's plan. We can't know what He knows. There are three "Omni" characteristics of God that we will never have. He is all-powerful (omnipotent), all-knowing (omniscient), and present everywhere (omnipresent).

Along with my new plan was a new attitude about my life and the people in it. As I learned, not everyone in my life was meant to stay. That was a painful thing for me to acknowledge because I assumed that everyone was meant to remain unless we had a falling out. That wasn't true. There have been people I considered terrific, close friends who faded out of my life. Most with no explanation or warning. By reading God's Word, I discovered that there are seasons for everything, and each season is designed to bring about growth and learning in your life. So it's important not to rush through a season because you're experiencing something painful. On the flip side, you shouldn't try and slow down a season because of something wonderful and pleasant that you don't want to end.

So, I embraced God's plan for my life and leaned into it. I made a conscious decision to grow and not be afraid to take my place in the Lord's Kingdom. I found a church home, started going consistently, and signed up for Bible study with small groups. As I've discovered with writing, if you want to learn more about your craft, hobbies, life, or God, you have to surround yourself with like-minded people because they will challenge you to grow and learn.

Being around Christians who shared my beliefs and goals was a balm to my battle-damaged soul. I was accepted, loved, and valued for exactly who I was—no changing to meet other people's needs was required. I was simply Lisa.

Praising and worshipping the Lord made me calm and happy. I made a conscious effort to put God at the center and not on the outskirts in no man's land like I'd been doing up until this point. By actively pursuing a closer relationship with the Lord, my habits and thinking shifted. My world no longer revolved around a spouse, so I had plenty of time for other pursuits. One area the Lord called me to was volunteering. Helping others was the warm blanket I needed to help my heart heal. Why? Because passing out lunches to school-aged children and meals and household supplies to adults in need gave me a chance to step outside of myself and my pain by focusing on the lives of others that needed my time more than I needed to wallow. It's almost impossible to feel down and glum when you're handing out meals, helping children, or giving back to your community. Using the gifts you were born with blesses not just those you are helping but also gives you the chance to utilize God-given talents. There are a few practical benefits to volunteering:

It makes you happy

Reduces stress

Allows you to connect with others

You are doing what Jesus did in his ministry

Provides an opportunity to sow into other's lives

Advances God's Kingdom

Serving others extends your life

"As each one has received a gift, minister it to one another, as good stewards of the manifold grace of God."[15]

Another bonus of serving was that it was hard to doubt myself while giving to people. I'm at my best when being selfless because we were created to be in relationships with others instead of focusing our attention inwardly or being alone.

The more effort I made to improve my spirituality, the more people came up to me with prophetic words for my life or provided me with a book or a piece of jewelry the Lord had impressed upon them to give me. I can't explain the peace and wonder I felt knowing God was wooing me to His side and reminding me through others just how much He loves His children.

The assignments that God places in your life may not always make sense to you or be what you envision for yourself, but if you trust in His Word and remain faithful to His plans, they will be far greater than those you could do on your own.

In the Bible, Rehoboam was the first king of the Kingdom of Judah. He was a son of and the successor to Solomon and a grandson of David.

---

15   1 Peter 4:10 (NKJV)

When King Rehoboam did things his way, situations didn't go so well for him. When he decided to listen to God, his circumstances turned around.

"Trust in the LORD with all your heart, And lean not on your own understanding; In all your ways acknowledge Him, And He shall direct your paths."[16]

Stop a moment and think of areas where your gifts can be of good use to help others and advance God's Kingdom. The Lord wants an active, daily relationship with you. And the more effort you make to have an intimate connection with Him, the more He will meet you where you are to make that happen.

Rehoboam Moment: When I began listening to the Lord's gentle promptings, the path before me grew wider. Take a moment and thank the Lord for His mercy, guidance, and Divine plan for your life. If you don't feel like you have a plan yet, ask the Holy Spirit to reveal it to you.

* * *

Deciding to follow God's plan for your life changes you. It requires sacrifice on your part by turning away from the things that come easy, your sinful nature, and the worldly things we all know and love. Following Jesus and putting Him first in your life takes re-dedicating yourself to the effort every day. We aren't perfect beings—only Jesus was without flaw.

There are days when I have the best intentions, but I can and do slip up sometimes because I'm born of sin. The farther I travel on my journey, the more I focus less on worldly things and more on what I gain through loving the Lord. That's not to say I don't sin because I do. Every day is a temptation, like a pork chop being waved in front of a hungry dog, but I have free will, and I make a choice whether or not I stray

---

16   Proverbs 3:5-6 (NKJV)

from the Lord that day. And if I do, I repent and ask for His forgiveness. I haven't touched that pork chop by the end of some days, and I happily celebrate that small victory. Dedicating your life to following Jesus and being Christlike isn't a free pass to a trial-free life. Just the opposite. You get tested, you're on the enemy's radar, and his demons know all about you. And they want nothing more than to put roadblocks along your path to keep you from Jesus and a new way of life. Those barriers can be glaringly apparent, like friends that may decide you've changed too much, and they don't want to be along for the ride.

If your spouse or significant other isn't a child of God, they may feel you're getting too wrapped up in going to church, Bible study, and your quest to live a different type of life. I remember a few conversations along those lines. There may also be subtle things that crop up to entice you to give this *new way of life* stuff up and go back to old behaviors.

After all, you've just put a target on your back in the spiritual realm, and the Devil would love nothing better than to derail your Christian walk. Do not let him succeed!

That's why it is crucial to study scriptures, read the Bible, and take up the armor of God because, like Job, you will be tested.

Job was a righteous, upright, and blameless Gentile who feared God and turned from evil. God allowed him to be tested by the enemy, and he was about as faithful as they came. Job lost everything. His beloved family, his station in life, his health, and more, yet he never wavered in his dedication to the Lord. Job was the best of men, and his devotion to God was legendary.

God would never leave you without the ability to defend yourself against your enemies. The Bible tells us to take up the armor of God, which is the *Belt of Truth*, the *Breastplate of Righteousness*, the *Gospel of Peace*, the *Shield of Faith*, the *Helmet of Salvation*, and the *Sword of the Spirit*.

"Finally, my brethren, be strong in the Lord and in the power of His might. Put on the whole armor of God, that you may be able to stand against the wiles of the devil. For we do not wrestle against flesh and blood, but against principalities, against powers, against the rulers

of the darkness of this age, against spiritual hosts of wickedness in the heavenly places. Therefore take up the whole armor of God, that you may be able to withstand in the evil day, and having done all, to stand. Stand therefore, having girded your waist with truth, having put on the breastplate of righteousness, and having shod your feet with the preparation of the gospel of peace; above all, taking the shield of faith with which you will be able to quench all the fiery darts of the wicked one. And take the helmet of salvation, and the sword of the Spirit, which is the word of God; praying always with all prayer and supplication in the Spirit, being watchful to this end with all perseverance and supplication for all the saints."[17]

Job Moment: *From scripture, we know there will always be challenges. When things in my life are at their worst, clinging to God's word is a light in the darkness. It provides me with the strength I need to overcome adversity. Is there an area in your life where you can take up your Armor of God today and let your power shine?*

---

17   Ephesians 6:10-18 (NKJV)

Chapter Eight

You Are Enough

Words, Pictures, Emotions, and Beliefs – *"The words you hear create pictures in your mind that, when attached to an emotion, become something you believe. This is the grid from which you begin to live your life."* — Pastor Lynton Turkington, Celebration Church

My Pastor made this statement during one of his sermons, and it has been impactful in my life. Recently, I've discovered that I have what it takes to persevere and continue growing because the Lord doesn't make mistakes. I am *exactly* the way I am for a reason. I'm not holding Him up, so I can't let Him down.

Granted, we inherit plenty of baggage from our parents, as they did from their parents, but do not believe that you can't break that cycle of generational curses. With God's help, you can and will.

It is also helpful not to believe what everyone tells you. Instead, consider what the Lord says about you. Keep from making negative declarations over your life like, *I'm never going to find love again, I'll never be good enough, smart enough, thin enough.*

Each of us is born with everything we need already inside to be whatever we choose to be. Resist the urge to become your worst enemy. Look to the Lord and ask Him to set you free from the musings of people who do not have your best interest at heart—yourself included. Let the Word of God, and not the word of man, be your stronghold on which your foundation stands.

My editor, and friend, Chandra Sparks Splond, was listening to me recently work through an upcoming project. During that call, I began listing all the things I needed to do and hadn't. She stopped me and said, "Lisa, you need to give yourself some grace."

That one sentence stopped me in my tracks and deflated the air from my rant on my shortcomings. Interestingly, I've said that same thing to other people who were in the middle of putting themselves down for what they saw as a deficit in themselves.

Love yourself the way God loves you. See yourself how He sees you.

We must remember that we are children of an awesome, powerful God, and He does not make mistakes. Each of us is unique. No one else has the combination of qualities, strengths, and attributes that make us who we are. We are born with everything we need for greatness. It just needs to be unlocked. So, for all of us that deflect when given a compliment and say, "Oh, this old thing ..." or, "Yeah, but it's only ..." Stop right there. Give *yourself* some grace. Don't beat yourself up, learn how to take a compliment, don't remind someone how average you are compared to other women or men. Do not start in about how far you still need to go, etc. Instead, sit and settle yourself into that praise and be grateful for it. We are made in God's image, and the Lord does not make mistakes. You are beautifully and fearfully made and exactly how God intended you to be. And if He is still working on some things in your life, let Him, because you will be the better for it. With patience comes great reward.

Celebrate your ability to continue to learn, grow, and experience life. Suppose there are things that you still want to do? Great. Go for it. Don't get stagnate, and cease moving forward. That would be a waste of the brains, gumption, and grit you inherited. Don't block your blessings. Embrace them.

Another thing I have learned recently is that forgiveness is not for *the other person*. It's for *you*.

Learn to walk in forgiveness. It would be best if you didn't spend all your time and energy holding grudges against others. No matter what was done to you. I had a breakthrough while in a Bible study class. We were discussing how God forgave our sins by the sacrifice of Jesus dying in our place. Our slate is wiped clean, and we are forgiven. God looks at His children through the blood of Jesus. So, who are we not to forgive others when the Lord forgave us? After that, I felt a release in my spirit. *Do not hold grudges*. Do not confront someone who has wronged you and tell them that *you* forgive *them* because it may not end how you expect. They may feel they have nothing to forgive. Then what? More anger? More animosity? It's safer to release the need to be validated through an apology. Instead, wouldn't it be wiser to forgive the trespasses of others as God forgave ours?

Joseph was one of Jacob's twelve sons. He was his favorite, and Jacob bestowed upon him a colorful coat that angered his brothers. They plotted to kill him and sold him into slavery. He was imprisoned, forgotten about, falsely accused of rape, and yet still held God's favor. Eventually, Joseph became one of Pharaoh's officials and wisely prevented famine in Egypt. Coming face-to-face with his brothers again, he forgave them and provided for his father, brothers, and families by relocating them to Egypt. Joseph could have been bitter about/over his early life, his family's betrayal, and the hardships Joseph endured. Instead, he was kind, forgiving, and learned humility and wisdom. Joseph never wavered in his trust in the Lord.

Scripture: *"But as for you, you meant evil against me; but God meant it for good, in order to bring it about as it is this day, to save many people alive."* [18]

Jacob Moment: *Are you holding on to unforgiveness in your heart? If so, ask the Holy Spirit to help you to release it so that you can heal and move on.*

Scripture: *"Delight yourself also in the L*ORD*, And He shall give you the desires of your heart."*[19]

This scripture in no way means that the Lord is a genie, and every earthly wish we make will be granted. Because let's face it, all of our desires may not be good or wise. Instead, delighting in the Lord means taking pleasure in Him more than we do other things in our lives. By having Him be first, God can shape and soften our hearts towards Him. By placing our needs and desires in His capable hands, we allow Him to provide for us. Our dependence lets us connect with the Lord in a more meaningful, intimate way. Let Him lead, and you follow because He can see what your spirit needs to thrive—your true heart's desire. It may not be that dream you were holding on to that you thought you needed to be happy. It could be something else entirely. But don't worry about the particulars. Instead, trust in the Lord. He's got this.

After my divorce, I had difficulty recalling what I liked, my favorite candle scent, hobby or, my heart's desires. Though I wasn't fearful about the lack of illumination, I was determined to figure it out. Between fulfilling the needs of my husband, my children, friends, and family, I kept deferring my wants and wishes. It was when I was alone that I finally took stock of some of these things. I realized that I was living everyone else's dream and not my own. I was the support staff, the cheerleader, and the miracle worker for them in a way that I had never been for myself. It is not that I am bitter or regret any decisions that I have made. However, this self-evaluation made me realize that I have to take care of myself, too. It is essential to feed my aspirations and hopes as I do for other people and not let myself get so depleted that I have nothing left for me.

---

18   Genesis 50:20 (NKJV)
19   Psalm 37:4 (NKJV)

This topic hit home when a woman of God prophesied over me at church. She said that the Lord wanted me to know He has not forgotten about the desires of my heart, and that I had been putting myself last in many ways and pushing aside the things I desired. The Lord also said those things would come to fruition and that He has not forgotten. She made the comparison to picking up a dandelion, making a wish, and then blowing it. God wanted me to know that He sees every one of those petals, and He sees every wish I have ever made. Wow, that's mind-boggling!

Elizabeth was the wife of the priest, Zechariah, and Mary's cousin. Elizabeth was old and unable to have children, but the angel Gabriel spoke to Zechariah and told him that they would soon be parents and name their baby John. While Zechariah questioned this, his wife did not. God knew what she desired most in her heart, and when He granted it to her, Elizabeth gave thanks to the Lord and accepted His gift.

Elizabeth Moment: Trust that God knows what you need most in your life. If someone or something is in your life and you wonder if it's God sent, ask Him. Pray about it and ask the Lord to let you know if it's from Him or just wishful thinking on your part. Say a prayer of re-dedication and put your life in His hands, and He will provide for all your needs. The Lord wants all of His children happy and fulfilled. And that starts first with trust.

What I have realized on my journey is that it is mine and unique—just like me. The Lord redirected my steps to take me off the path I had placed myself on by not running my choices, wants, and desires through God's filter instead of my own. I listened to my heart, feelings, and the material world to direct my steps, not the Creator of all life. That's the equivalent of listening to someone telling you the gist of a movie without you seeing it for yourself, and you be satisfied with their version instead of your own experience. Some things can get lost in the translation.

We are meant to experience life to the fullest, helping and loving others as we love ourselves. The last two years of my life have allowed me to breathe, exhale, regroup, and refocus. Why? Because I had been through the emotional, mental, and relationship wringer, and I came out on the other side intact and a whole lot happier than I went in.

I survived divorce, gained my independence, and discovered a long-dormant thing called grit. Do you know the first thing I did when my young adults and I moved into our new place? After blessing it, I lit candles. And not just the plain vanilla candles that I was used to because my ex-husband had a sensitive nose and didn't like too many different smells. But crazy wild scents that you'd never think went together, like Lavender Lemonade or Red Lava Citrus.

Flowers were next on my be-free-and-happy list: floral arrangements, floral clothing, floral paintings. See the pattern here? I had willingly deferred my wishes, wants, and needs. So while I was unpacking boxes and figuring out where my life's possessions were going to go, I blew the dust off and put myself right out in the open to bask in God's glory where I belonged.

Nelson Mandela said, "It always seems impossible until it's done."

Being divorced seemed impossible. Living on my own with my kids looked impossible. Rediscovering myself after years of drifting through life in a fog sounded impossible. Finding my spiritual gifts and putting them to good use felt impossible—until it was done.

I am enjoying my life and relishing each day as an opportunity to discover something new about myself that I didn't know. It's like unpacking an unexpected gift from God each day—and I love surprises.

Dating? Sure, at some point. Marriage? Why not? But I'm in no rush because I can finally see a glimmer of the path that Jesus chose for me before I was even born.

It fills me with excitement to begin this new journey because I'm not alone—I never was. My foundation is rebuilt, and now it's unbreakable because God fortifies it. With Him as my compass, I know my direction is true, and my future is bright because *"Your word is a lamp to my feet And a light to my path."*[20]

With Him, all things are possible—I just needed to believe it and take this journey of discovery with Him by accepting His heart, seeking His face, and living the life He intended for me. And that's the gist of what God has been trying to show me all along.

---

20   Psalm 119:105 (NKJV)

Author's Note:

Thank you for reading! I hope that you enjoyed my story in this series. Writing Journey allowed me the freedom and room to experience the Holy Spirit working through me. While penning the fiction element based on the actual Bible characters in the Book of Ruth, I was able to connect with her story in a way I had not done before. It was healing for me to take my life experiences as they tied into the theme of this book and relay how the Lord helped me along my path to healing and a closer connection to Him.

Want to know how to let Jesus into your life?

If you do not know the Lord as your Savior but are ready to give your life to Him, here are a few steps you can take:

Seek forgiveness for your sins—the Salvation Prayer.

" that if you confess with your mouth the Lord Jesus and believe in your heart that God has raised Him from the dead, you will be saved. For with the heart one believes unto righteousness, and with the mouth confession is made unto salvation. "[21]

Make the Lord the center of your life, and ask Holy Spirit to help you achieve this goal.

Pray

Read the Word of God (the Bible)

Participate in Praise and Worship

Do not go it alone. Seek other children of God to be around for support, learning, and growth.

About the Author

National Bestselling, and Amazon #1 bestselling author, Lisa Dodson, has written over seventeen novels in the Multicultural, Contemporary, Romantic Suspense, Sweet Romance, and Clean Read genres. Lisa writes positive, realistic characters that she hopes readers can connect with while enjoying her novels.

She has functioned in the literary community as a publicist and radio talk show host. Lisa also works with both aspiring and published authors in marketing and content editing.

Connect with Lisa https://sociatap.com/LisaDodson

The Merry Hearts Inspirational Series will warm your heart and touch your soul . . .

Clean Romantic Suspense

Alejandro "Dro" Reyes has been a "fixer" for as long as he could remember, which makes owning a crisis management company focused on repairing professional reputations the perfect fit. The same could be said of Lola Samuels, who is only vaguely aware of his true talents and seems oblivious to the growing attraction between them. His company, Vantage Point, is in high demand, and business in the Windy City is booming. Until a mysterious call following an attempt on his mentor's life forces him to drop everything and accept a fated position with The Castle, which blindsides him with an enemy he never saw coming. Public relations maven, Lola Samuels, has just been given an impossible task to fix the tarnished image of longtime bad boy, Shawn Mayhew. She reaches out to Dro for assistance, unaware of the underlying tension between the Mayhews and Reyes families. What starts as a cut and dry working arrangement becomes complicated by danger, ulterior motives, and a love that won't be denied. When Alejandro discovers the lengths that the Mayhews will go to unseat him and ruin his family, who has a decades-long affiliation to The Castle, he calls in a few reinforcements of his own from his brother Kings.

But there's a hidden agenda that Alejandro doesn't see coming who threatens his life, his woman, and his throne.

Excerpt – *King of Hyde Park*

Lola smoothed her hands over the royal blue square neck sheath dress draped across her curvy body. It was the first time she'd worn cap sleeves. She always thought the cut made her arms look big, but Michelle assured her that she looked fierce. Her shoulder-length, brown hair was swept into a messy bun with wisps framing her face. Running late, she'd grabbed her black tortoiseshell glasses instead of contact lenses.

In need of an extra boost of confidence since getting off on the wrong foot, Lola made sure that her hair, makeup, and outfit were firing on all cylinders. She peeped down at her blush Ferragamo pumps. From the moment she'd spotted them in a magazine, she'd loved them. She'd commented to her mother how beautiful they were.

Lola was genuinely surprised months later when her mother, Maggie Samuels, presented them on her birthday.

"Mom, these shoes are almost half the rent on my apartment."

"Yes, they are," her mother had observed with a wide smile. *"But you're our only daughter, who else do we have to spoil?"*

Lola couldn't argue with that logic. Besides, she didn't want to. She loved her parents. She loved her shoes. Though she'd only worn them three times, this being the third. She knew it was crazy, but she always felt like nobody could say no to her when she wore them. She called them her Cinderella heels.

The intercom buzzed on her desk phone.

"Mr. Alejandro Reyes is here to see you, Miss Samuels," her assistant Jess replied.

"Thanks, Jess, show him in."

A moment later, she ushered Dro through the door. Jess stood aside as he sauntered in.

Lola was standing by the window, so she had to walk across the full length of her office. He didn't appear to be in a hurry, so she took her time, too. It gave her time to appreciate how good he looked dressed in a dark gray suit, blue and white striped shirt, a dark blue silk tie, and black shoes. He exuded so much masculinity he could've poured it into a cup.

Her assistant gazed at him, and then to Lola. She mouthed the words, "*Oh my gosh.*" Held her hand to her forehead as though taking her temperature and faked a swoon.

Lola had to work hard not to burst out laughing. She gave her assistant a stern stare before she said, "Thank you, Jess."

"My pleasure, Miss Samuels. Shall I hold all your calls?" She asked, trying to linger.

"Yes, thank you."

"Of course," she stressed before turning to leave. She stopped short, almost throwing herself off-balance in the process. "Would you care for some coffee, Mr. Reyes? We also have tea, soda, bottled water?"

He turned around and gave Jess his full consideration. Lola noticed that her assistant looked as though she would truly pass out from his undivided attention.

"I'm good, thank you, Jess," he said with a lazy smile.

Her assistant stood there a full three seconds as if she'd forgotten her name.

Lola's eyebrows crept into her hairline. "Jess?"

"Hmm? Oh, sorry about that." She blushed and laughed at herself as she hightailed it out of the room, closing the door behind her.

Lola could understand Jess' momentary lapse of professionalism. It had been a while since she'd seen him in person. If at all possible, her memory hardly did him justice. Even with her heels, he was taller, and she was five feet, ten inches.

It also caused her a little embarrassment to know that her dream Dro was almost spot on with the man in person. His dimples, the flecks of gold in his brown eyes, even his luscious mane of thick, jet black hair was jaw-dropping.

Lola had to keep her hands fisted at her sides to stave off the desire to touch the wisps of hair falling across his forehead.

He had the kind of looks that caused a woman to place a hand over her heart without even being aware she'd done it. And his voice only added to his appeal. Dro never rushed to do anything, especially not to speak. He was reserved, and always calculating with his words. And he had the fiercest poker face she'd ever seen. He never gave away what he was thinking. He was notorious for it.

Clearing her throat, Lola said, "My apologies, please, have a seat." She motioned to the conference table in the corner.

He followed behind her and pulled out her chair before taking a seat himself. He crossed his leg at the ankle and unbuttoned his jacket in one fluid motion. He motioned for her to begin.

"I thought I'd start with a quick background on my work here—"

"No need," he interrupted. "You've been working at Mayhew Industries for a little over three years now. You beat out hundreds of applicants for the coveted position as Director of Public Relations. Before that, you worked at a boutique PR firm across town, as director, and before that, a firm in Evanston as a junior partner. You left both when you were passed over for promotion in favor of your white, male counterparts. You graduated at the top of your class from the University of Illinois at Urbana-Champaign. You're originally from Alexandria, Virginia, where your parents still live. At least half the year. They have a condo here in Chicago not far from you in the Gold Coast neighborhood. You're an only child, never married, no children, or pets."

Lola took a few seconds to process how he had summed up her life. "Are you going to tell me about my financial investments, too?" She joked.

"Did you want me to?"

Clean Romantic Suspense

A tell-all novel, a stalker, and a checklist of suspects have debut author Sasha Lambert trying to determine what's fact or fiction.

The Passport Diaries is an instant hit, but Sasha's ex-boyfriend, Milo Georgopoulos thinks it's all about their relationship and airing his dirty laundry. He gives Sasha an ultimatum: Ditch the book or else.

Entrepreneur and former athlete Pierce Deveraux thinks he too has been placed between the pages of Sasha's novel. Determined to make Sasha pay for putting a ding in his knight-in-shining-armor image, Pierce contemplates how best to even the score. When strange things begin happening wherever Sasha goes, even her twin sister, Dr. Sienna Lambert-Deveraux, worries for her safety.

With an adoring assistant, an ambitious publicist, and a jealous ex-lover vying for her attention, Sasha soon finds herself at the center of a dangerous tug-of-war.

Excerpt from *Interview with Danger*

"Pierce, what's going on?"

"That's exactly what I'd like to know," he growled. "Have you lost your mind, Sasha? Do you know what you've done?"

She stared at him blankly. "I don't understand. Will you stop beating around the bush and tell me the problem?"

"*You* are the problem," he threw back. "You and your stupid book have ruined my life, Sasha…and you'd better believe you're going to fix it."

Her mouth dropped open. "I don't have a clue what you're talking about."

"Jacob Toliver."

Sasha waited, but Pierce didn't say anything else. Instead, he moved closer until he was crowding her. He folded his arms across his chest and stared at her. Finally, she threw her hands up. "What, are we playing twenty questions?"

"Jacob Toliver," he repeated.

Sasha pinched the bridge of her nose. "I know who he is. I wrote the book, remember? I'm just wondering what my character has to do with this."

"He's me."

Sasha's eyebrows rose. "You…you think Jacob…is you?" She started to laugh, then pushed past him to go into the lounge. "He isn't you, Pierce."

He was right on her heels.

"Well, there are some people that disagree with you. In fact, the executives at the sporting goods store that just dropped me as an endorser would beg to differ…and the men's apparel ad I was going to do and—"

"I don't understand."

"Apparently, a few of them read your book and thought your midnight Casanova was me. You just cost me three quarters of a million dollars," Pierce said between clenched teeth.

Her smile faded. "What?"

"Yeah, that's what I said. Apparently, they didn't want a womanizing, strung-out playboy representing their brands. Considering these are family businesses, I can understand why," he snapped.

She eyed him from head to toe. "Well, are you?"

His expression turned indignant. "Certainly not."

"Then there you go." Sasha threw up her hands in frustration. "Pierce, this is absurd. You could throw a stick and hit thousands of men that fit that same description."

"You know, your sister tried to say that, too. Obviously, the list is a lot smaller than either of you think," he said dryly.

"Your claim is ridiculous. Why would anyone think it's you?" The corners of her mouth elevated slightly.

He glowered at her. "You think this is funny?"

"No," she answered, instantly contrite. "I'm sorry. It's just that your accusations are outrageous."

"Outrageous? My image has been damaged, and it's your fault, Sasha. Do you know how hard I've worked to get back to where I was and just like that—"

"Wait, what do you mean back?"

"In less than three hundred pages," he continued, ignoring her question, "of some smutty book it's gone."

Anger propelled her forward until she was in his face, her finger pointing at his chest. "Now wait a minute. Have you read it?"

"Are you kidding me?"

"Then you shouldn't comment on things you know nothing about," she shot back. "My book is not smutty. It has real merit, and it's now a *USA Today* bestseller."

"Really? Well, I hope it's worth six figures, sweetheart, because I've got a mind to sue you for slander."

Sasha was shaking with rage. "For the last time, I did not use you as the basis for my character, Pierce. In case you hadn't realized it, I used to be a flight attendant, and my ex-boyfriend was a multi-millionaire… is," she corrected. "Needless to say, I've traveled to quite a few places."

"Your exploits with a married man don't concern me." Pierce's voice dripped with sarcasm.

The dig got under her skin, making her want to lash out. "The point is I've been all over the world, and I've met dozens of Jacob Tolivers in my travels, and trust me, *you* aren't that original."

Before he could respond to her not-so-veiled insult, a loud crash sounded behind them, followed by a deafening boom that shook the house. Pierce grabbed Sasha by the shoulders and hurled her to the floor, using his body to shield her. A startled scream escaped Sasha's lips. Smoke filled the air, causing them both to cough. She attempted to move, but Pierce had her locked down like a vice.

Sasha's eyes felt like they were on fire. Instinctively, she slammed them shut. After a few seconds of silence, she assumed the danger had abated and pushed Pierce again to try and get up.

"Keep still," he commanded. With Pierce's face buried in her hair, his voice came out muffled. "Is there another exit?"

She opened her eyes to look at him and instantly regretted it. Tears ran down her face, blinding her almost as much as the searing pain in her eyes.

"What?" She coughed.

"We need another way out," Pierce said urgently.

"My eyes are killing me—"

"I know. But, we need get out of here. Think, Sasha."

"Oh…the…the patio."

"Let's go." Pierce reached out and grasped her hand. "Stay low. It's less smoke closer to the ground. "Hold your breath as much as you can."

"Wait. We'll get there faster if I lead," she said in a raspy voice.

"Fair enough. Get moving."

Sasha crawled toward the French doors with Pierce right on her tail. She almost cried with relief when she reached out and felt the wood frame. "We're here," she choked out.

Pierce raised himself up just high enough to open one of the doors. He pushed on her back gently so that she got the hint to go through. Once they were clear, both collapsed onto the brick patio. Using his foot,

Pierce kicked the door closed behind them. Each struggled to breathe in hungry gulps of clean air, which only caused another fit of coughing.

"Water hose?" he rasped out.

Trying to control the wracking coughs, Sasha pointed to the far wall.

Pierce staggered across the patio to turn on the spigot. With a few tugs, he was able to pull the garden hose over to Sasha.

"Here." He knelt in front of her, motioning for her to hold out her hands. When she complied, he sprayed water so she could splash her face. When that wasn't going fast enough, he doused her with the hose from head to toe before doing the same to himself.

"I'm good," she sputtered after a few minutes.

Sasha sat back and wiped the excess water from her face. Luckily, it was warm out and the water was cool, but not freezing.

Pierce returned the hose to its place. When he got back, he helped Sasha to her feet. She swayed a moment, but he steadied her.

"Thanks," she whispered.

Soaking wet and wreaking of smoke, they plopped down on patio chairs. Pierce regarded Sasha through bloodshot eyes.

"You okay?"

"Better now," she croaked.

"You look like a drowned cat."

For a moment, Sasha looked offended. Finally, her mouth tilted into a smirk. "So do you, though a lot bigger…actually, more like a drowned mountain lion."

Pierce got to his feet. "Stay here," he told her before disappearing back into the house.

With cautious movements, he eased his way to the front door and peered out through the massive hole that used to be a decorative glass window. There were bystanders gathering on the sidewalk, and he heard sirens in the distance.

"Do you see anything?"

Pierce spun around. "I thought I told you to stay outside."

With a huff, Sasha's expression darkened. "I'm not much for doing what I'm told."

"Clearly," he grumbled. "How are your eyes?"

"Better, but they still hurt like the devil, and my throat burns."

He looked around at the mess. "I guess that was someone's idea of a prank. The cops will be here soon." Pierce strode over and kicked the used container lying in the middle of the floor. Lowering himself on his haunches, he took a closer look.

He was still surveying the area when Sasha returned with a dishtowel.

"What's that?" she asked, moving closer and handing him the cloth.

"Some sort of smoke canister, along with a huge rock they used to lob it through the glass on your front door." He wiped the remaining water off his face. "If we'd been standing here," he said, pointing, "one of us would have a real bad headache—or worse."

The color drained from her face as his words hit home.

Pierce extended his hand. "I found this, too."

Sasha retrieved the wrinkled piece of paper and read it. She met his gaze. "It says…find another hobby."

"I know. I read it. Clearly this wasn't a prank after all."

"Are you sure?"

He stared at her as though she'd lost her mind. "Are you kidding?"

Sasha shook her head. "First scorpions, and now this."

That got Pierce's attention. He turned and stared at Sasha. "Did you say…scorpions?"

"It's a long story," she began, but pounding on the front door interrupted her. She rushed to let the police in, and a whirlwind of activity began.

Pierce glanced around the room to take in all the men coming in and out, then gazed back to Sasha. "It appears we've got plenty of time."

Sasha let out a long, ragged sigh. Inching closer to Pierce, she wrapped her arms protectively around herself while they surveyed the chaos. "I just don't understand," she choked out. "Who would do something like this?"

Pierce shrugged while watching events unfold around them. "Apparently someone else you've pissed off."

www.ingramcontent.com/pod-product-compliance
Lightning Source LLC
Chambersburg PA
CBHW011943050726

47590CB00011B/3331